FUN FACT FILE: WORLD WONDERS!

20 FUN FACTS ABOUT MACHU PICCHU

By Janey Levy

Gareth Stevens
Publishing

Please visit our website, www.garethstevens.com. For a free color catalog of all our high-quality books, call toll free 1-800-542-2595 or fax 1-877-542-2596.

Library of Congress Cataloging-in-Publication Data

Levy, Janey.
20 fun facts about Machu Picchu / by Janey Levy.
 p. cm. — (Fun fact file: world wonders)
Includes index.
ISBN 978-1-4824-0455-5 (pbk.)
ISBN 978-1-4824-0456-2 (6-pack)
ISBN 978-1-4824-0452-4 (library binding)
1. Machu Picchu Site (Peru) — Juvenile literature. 2. Incas — History — Juvenile literature. 3. Inca architecture — Juvenile literature.I. Levy, Janey. II. Title.
F3429.1.M3 L48 2014
985.019—dc23

First Edition

Published in 2014 by
Gareth Stevens Publishing
111 East 14th Street, Suite 349
New York, NY 10003

Copyright © 2014 Gareth Stevens Publishing

Designer: Sarah Liddell
Editor: Greg Roza

Photo credits: Cover, p. 1 Danita Delimont/Gallo Images/Getty Images; p. 5 kccullenPhoto/Shutterstock.com; p. 6 Richard I'Anson/Lonely Planet Images/Getty Images; p. 7 Amy Allcock/Flickr/Getty Images; p. 8 Richard Bergmann/Photo Researchers/Getty Images; p. 9 Leemage/Universal Images Group/Getty Images; pp. 10, 21 Jarno Gonzalez Zarraonandia/Shutterstock.com; p. 11 Spanish School/The Bridgeman Art Library/Getty Images; p. 12 tr3gin/Shutterstock.com; p. 13 Narongsak Nagadhana/Shutterstock.com; p. 14 Achim Baque/Shutterstock.com; p. 15 photo courtesy of Wikimedia Commons, Karta MachuPicchu.png; p. 16 Neale Cousland/Shutterstock.com; p. 17 alltoz696/Shutterstock.com; p. 18 Galyna Andrushko/Shutterstock.com; p. 19 Stephen Collector/Photolibrary/Getty Images; p. 20 © J. L. Levy; p. 22 American School/The Bridgeman Art Library/Getty Images; p. 23 Andre Distel Photography/Flickr/Getty Images; p. 24 Tracy Packer Photography/Flickr/Getty Images; p. 25 photo courtesy of Wikimedia Commons, Hiram Bingham at Machu Piccu ruins 1911.jpg; p. 26 J. L. Levy/Shutterstock.com; p. 27 photo courtesy of Wikimedia Commons, Machupicchu hb10.jpg; p. 29 Nika Lerman/Shutterstock.com.

Printed in the United States of America

CPSIA compliance information: Batch #CW14GS: For further information contact Gareth Stevens, New York, New York at 1-800-542-2595.

Contents

Words in the glossary appear in **bold** type the first time they are used in the text.

City in the Clouds

Imagine a city so high in the mountains it's called the city in the clouds. That's Machu Picchu. Located in the South American country of Peru, this centuries-old Incan city sits high in the cloud-covered Andes Mountains.

The steep slopes and **tropical** mountain forests make it hard to reach Machu Picchu. And that's part of the city's mystery and wonder. Who were the Inca? What was the city like? How did they build here? Why did they choose this location? Keep reading to find out!

Machu Picchu was built about 550 years ago.

FACT 1

At first, the early Inca were just an ordinary small Andean tribe.

The Inca became more powerful when they started attacking nearby tribes in the early 1300s. They began building their great empire in the early 1400s. The emperor at that time was Viracocha Inca, whose name means "Creator God Ruler."

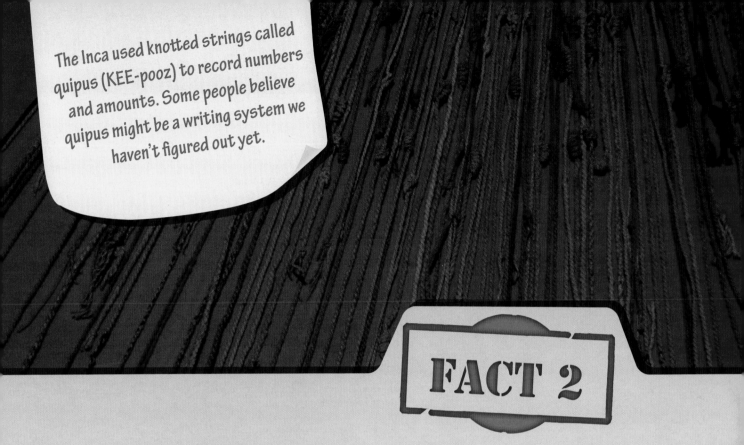

The Inca used knotted strings called quipus (KEE-pooz) to record numbers and amounts. Some people believe quipus might be a writing system we haven't figured out yet.

FACT 2

Although the Inca built a great empire, they had no writing system.

Like other Andean societies, the Inca left no written records. Their history was kept by official "memorizers," who learned it by heart and passed it down through the years. When Spanish **conquistadors** arrived in 1532, they recorded what they heard from the memorizers.

FACT 3

The Inca built an empire with very simple tools.

The Inca Empire ran about 2,500 miles (4,020 km) from north to south and had a population of about 12 million. Amazingly, the Inca created one of the world's largest empires without basic instruments, such as iron or steel tools and the wheel.

The Inca built 10,000 miles (16,000 km) of roads. But ordinary people couldn't use them. The roads were just for government and military business.

Francisco Pizarro, shown here, led the Spanish soldiers who arrived in Peru in 1532.

The Inca Empire lasted only about 100 years.

Around 1527, the Incan emperor died, and war followed. While the Inca were fighting each other, Spanish conquistadors arrived and brought the empire to an end. But the Inca had created wonders while the empire lasted. Perhaps the greatest wonder was Machu Picchu.

Fit for a King

Machu Picchu was a royal estate.

Construction on Machu Picchu began around 1450. It was a place the emperor, Pachacuti Inca Yupanqui, and his family could go to rest. Servants lived there all the time, prepared the **estate** for the emperor's visits, and served him while he was there.

Pachacuti Inca Yupanqui, whose name means "He Who Remakes the World," occupied the royal palace when he was at Machu Picchu.

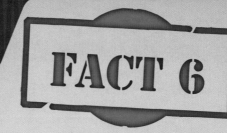

FACT 6

Even after Pachacuti Inca Yupanqui died, he still owned Machu Picchu.

Pachacuti was mummified after his death in 1471. This was the usual Incan practice. The emperor's mummy was honored, asked for advice, and given food and drink daily. The crops from his estate were meant to provide for his mummy, servants, and family forever.

During the Inca Empire, mummies of emperors were carried in parades on special occasions.

FACT 7

Visiting Machu Picchu might make you sick.

Machu Picchu is about 8,000 feet (2,440 m) above sea level. At that **altitude**, there's less oxygen in the air, which could give you altitude sickness. You might have a headache, have trouble breathing, be very tired, and feel like throwing up.

The Andes mountain range has some of the tallest mountains in the world. It's also the world's longest range, running about 4,500 miles (7,240 km) down the western coast of South America.

The stones used to build Machu Picchu came from the very spot where the city was built.

FACT 8

Machu Picchu covers an area about twice the size of Washington, DC.

Machu Picchu covers about 125 square miles (325 sq km). Within that area are more than 200 buildings and more than 700 **terraces**. The terraces, on the mountain slopes surrounding the city, take up much of the area. The city itself is much smaller.

Map of Machu Picchu

The map of Machu Picchu on page 15 shows buildings and terraces at the top of the mountain. It also shows the Urubamba River, which flows through the valley far below Machu Picchu.

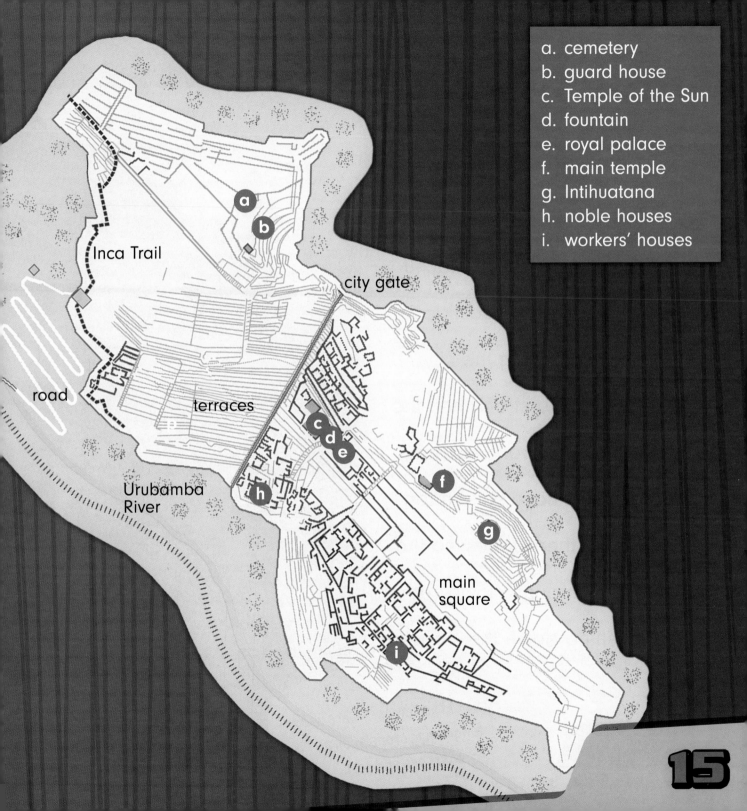

a. cemetery
b. guard house
c. Temple of the Sun
d. fountain
e. royal palace
f. main temple
g. Intihuatana
h. noble houses
i. workers' houses

Inca Trail

city gate

road

terraces

Urubamba
River

main
square

15

The terraces were built to hold up the mountain.

Heavy rainfall at Machu Picchu can cause mudslides. Before constructing the city, builders had to strengthen the mountain to prevent **erosion**. The terraces have soil on top, then sand, then stones, so the rain flows through slowly rather than rushing down the slopes.

Some of the terraces were used for growing crops such as potatoes and corn.

Many drains carried water to the central square, or plaza, shown here. The plaza was built with stones below the soil, just like in the terraces, to drain water away slowly.

FACT 10

You can't see more than half of the construction at Machu Picchu because it's underground.

Underground, the builders constructed **foundations** for the buildings and a **drainage system** to carry rainwater away from the city. The drainage system reaches almost 9 feet (2.7 m) below the surface and includes more than 100 drains throughout the city.

The building stones aren't all the same size or shape, but they fit together perfectly.

FACT 11

The building stones at Machu Picchu fit tightly together without the use of mortar.

Even without iron or steel tools, the Inca shaped building stones so exactly that they fit tightly together and didn't need **mortar** to hold them in place. The stones fit together so closely you can't put a knife blade between them.

18

Sometimes, the stones in Machu Picchu's buildings "dance."

Machu Picchu is in an area where **earthquakes** occur. During an earthquake, the stones bounce around, then fall back into place. If mortar were holding the stones together, they couldn't do this, and the buildings would have fallen down long ago.

This stone doorway is still standing after hundreds of years.

Today, visitors to Machu Picchu can see the royal palace, including the stone platform where the emperor had his bed and the emperor's private toilet.

royal palace

Temple of the Sun

fountain

FACT 13

The emperor had the only private bath and private toilet at Machu Picchu.

Naturally, the emperor had the best of everything. In addition to a private bath and toilet, he had a garden. His palace was near the first fountain, so he got the purest drinking water. It was also next to one of the main temples.

Some believe the Inca built Machu Picchu here because the spot is sacred.

The Inca worshipped the sun, rivers, and mountains as gods. They also believed they gained power from being close to **sacred** locations. Four sacred mountains surround Machu Picchu, and the sacred Urubamba River in the valley below curls around the mountain.

The sacred Intihuatana stone, shown here, was used to study the sun. Its name means "where the sun is tied."

21

FACT 15

Machu Picchu was abandoned around 1550.

No one is sure why, but the Inca abandoned, or deserted, Machu Picchu around 1550. Some say the cause was sickness or lack of water. Some say it was because of the war among the Inca. Others say it was because of the Spanish conquistadors.

This picture shows a battle between the Inca and the Spanish.

Machu Picchu was never finished.

Builders had been working at Machu Picchu about 100 years when it was abandoned. Pachacuti Inca Yupanqui had been dead more than 60 years. But the city was still not completed. Finished stones ready to be put into place lie all around the city.

In addition to the stones on the ground, another sign Machu Picchu wasn't finished are stones that were put into place but never received the final finishing touches they should have.

The Spanish conquistadors may have brought a quick end to the Inca Empire, but they never found Machu Picchu.

The Spanish found and destroyed other major Incan cities, but they didn't reach Machu Picchu. Some say it's because the Inca destroyed all bridges on the road to Machu Picchu so the Spanish couldn't get there.

Visitors today may choose to travel to Machu Picchu the way the Inca did—by hiking the Inca Trail.

Machu Picchu remained largely forgotten until Hiram Bingham "discovered" it in 1911.

University professor Hiram Bingham made Machu Picchu known around the world, but the city was already well known to local people. Local farmers led Bingham to the place. He arrived to see people farming on some of Machu Picchu's terraces.

Hiram Bingham

Machu Picchu was overgrown by the forest when Bingham found it.

Machu Picchu isn't the city's real name, but no one is sure what the Inca called it.

Local people called the city Machu Picchu because that's the name of the mountain. It means "old mountain" or "old peak." Opposite this peak is a shorter one named Huayna Picchu, which means "young mountain" or "young peak."

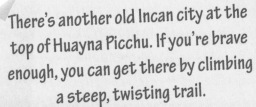

There's another old Incan city at the top of Huayna Picchu. If you're brave enough, you can get there by climbing a steep, twisting trail.

Bingham always believed he'd found Vilcabamba. He wasn't proved wrong until after his death in 1956.

FACT 20

Bingham never really knew what he'd found.

Bingham had been looking for Vilcabamba, the "lost city of the Inca." The last Incan emperors fought the Spanish from there. The conquistadors captured Vilcabamba in 1572, but they never recorded where it was. That's why it became the "lost city."

A World Wonder

The Inca created Machu Picchu as a grand estate for their emperor. They constructed it to last for centuries. If the Spanish had found it, they would likely have destroyed it. It's our good fortune they didn't.

Machu Picchu was named a World **Heritage** Site in 1983 and one of the New Seven Wonders of the World in 2007. Every year, hundreds of thousands of people from around the world visit the city in the clouds. Perhaps one day you'll have the chance to see it in person!

Much of Machu Picchu has been restored to its original state over the years.

Glossary

altitude: height above sea level

conquistador: a Spanish soldier who came to the Americas in the 1500s to find land and riches

drainage system: a system built to carry water away from an area

earthquake: a powerful shaking of Earth caused by the movement of pieces of Earth's crust

erosion: the wearing away or shaping of Earth's land by wind, water, and ice

estate: land with a large, usually fancy, house

foundation: the underground base or support for a building

heritage: something handed down from the past

mortar: cement or other matter that is used to hold bricks or stones together

sacred: special to the gods

terrace: one of a series of narrow, flat strips of land that go up a hill or mountain like steps

tropical: having to do with the warm areas of Earth near the equator

For More Information

Books

Croy, Anita. *Solving the Mysteries of Machu Picchu.* New York, NY: Marshall Cavendish Benchmark, 2009.

Kops, Deborah. *Machu Picchu.* Minneapolis, MN: Twenty-First Century Books, 2009.

Newman, Sandra. *The Inca Empire.* New York, NY: Children's Press, 2010.

Websites

Inca Civilization
www.brainpop.com/socialstudies/worldhistory/incacivilization/preview.weml
Learn facts about the Inca and Machu Picchu, and watch a movie about Incan civilization.

Inca Empire: Machu Picchu
www.ducksters.com/history/inca/machu_picchu.php
Learn where, when, why, and how Machu Picchu was built, and view a map of the ruins.

Peru
kids.nationalgeographic.com/kids/places/find/peru/
Learn about Peru and its history, see photos and a map, and watch a video.

Index